Dedication

To all the people who have been amazing to me; a big thank-you, and an equal thank-you to those who have been less than amazing; thank you for the lessons and for giving me the courage to be the person I am today!

Contents

Introduction

So, just like you, I was stuck in relationships which were 50% pleasure and 50% hardship. Then, later on, maybe 70% pleasure and 30% hardship. Neither is good enough.

We all deserve and should aim for 95-98% pleasure and 2-5% space for improvement.

And, just like you, I thought I was very intelligent, had class, was well educated, was fun, was very attractive and could not understand why I was attracting emotionally unavailable men or men with too much emotional baggage, and why I just couldn't settle down and be happy in a stable, loving relationship.

I did realize, however, that my ratio of pleasure and hardship kept changing, depending on how much I loved, valued and respected myself.

So, I started digging into it and realized the following:

- I can have a perfect relationship if I can imagine one and believe I deserve one
- I have to be very exact and specific about what I want in my ideal partner
- If I take responsibility for all my thoughts, emotions and actions I can get what I want every single time
- I must persist and be resilient in order to get what I want in life

- **And mainly:**

    All my previous relationship failures happened because of the way I was programmed.

    Now you are probably wondering, "What is she talking about?"

    And this is the biggest secret behind any unhappiness, lack of success, failure and frustration...

    From the time we were born, up until the age of 5 to 7 years, we were programmed by our parents, grandparents and teachers to behave in a particular way.

    We were in a constant state of hypnosis, where we were like sponges soaking up all available information to later make sense of how life works on this planet.

It was our parents saying things like:

- Don't touch this, you will get burned
- Stop running, you will fall
- You cannot have chocolate now
- No, I cannot buy you a new toy
- I do not print the money

- Stop eating donuts; you will get fat
- Stop crying; you don't have a reason to
- Be quiet; you are giving me a headache
- Be nice to everyone
- Don't fight with other girls and boys…
  you catch my drift, I'm sure.

And, of course, *they* started programming us for our later relationships:

- How *they* behaved towards their partner
- What *they* thought of the opposite sex
- Why Mommy is crying
- Why Daddy is screaming at Mommy
- Why *they* are arguing or fighting
- Why *they* are not speaking and look angry
- Mommy saying all men are horrible, bullies or cheaters
- Mommy screaming at father for not making enough money to provide for his family
- Is Mommy nice to Daddy?
- Does Mommy smile and look happy?
- Does Mommy make a nice dinner?
- Does Daddy say "Thank you for a lovely meal"?
- Is any of that my fault? etc.

And all this resulted in us buying into how they perceived life and relationships.

So, when someone says "All men are horrible, nasty creatures who only think of sex", as a child that information (or any other information you have heard from your parents) will stick with you, and will make you fear men and expect the possibility of you finding the same kind of men, because the Mommy you so trust and love and are dependent on told you so, so clearly it must be true.

But all your Mom did was tell you *her* personal experience and not the universal truth.

Because guess what?! There are hundreds of millions of lovely, caring, loving, affectionate, protective, kind and adorable men around!

The fact that your Mom did not find one, was dependent on her own programming, *not* on the truth.

So, the only thing you need to do now is to find out what your programming is and change it.

We call that "programming" or "rewiring" the brain.

It means taking all your negative beliefs about **life, love, relationships, men and you**, throwing them as far as you can and installing new beneficial positive beliefs which will *get you what you want*.

And if you do that, I guarantee you that you will not just attract, but *create* the man you want and live in a permanent loyal, happy relationship forever.

CHAPTER 1

It's All about You!

Your wish is your command.

Yes, you *CAN* have the perfect partner and the perfect relationship!

I can say it because I know so and all my clients live it.

And my mission is to show you how.

Have you noticed the women who marry 3, 4 or 5 times, each time attracting the same characteristics and 'short-comings' in their mate?

Or all the women who keep saying they cannot find a nice man, because they either are not available or believe that most men are just horrible?

I have breaking news for you, listen very carefully!

We have this amazing thing called the brain. It is our most devoted friend. It means well and literally acts as our servant. It was built to execute absolutely everything we say to it.

So, if I have a donut and I say to myself that I will gain weight because donuts have that power over me, my brain heard me saying it and, because it is obligated to execute all my wishes – meaning literally everything I think and say, it will make me gain weight, because it trusts the information I gave to be my personal wish.

Hence, if I tell my brain that all men are horrible and good men are not available…guess what? it **has to** make that happen for me!

The brain will always find me more of what I believe. So, my own brain will find more horrible men and will put me in all sorts of situations which will prove to me, beyond any reasonable doubt, that good men do not exist. And if they do, they are either married or taken.

Can you see now how the behaviour of others is not random, that it is literally dictated by you and your brain?

So, the only thing you need to do to get your ideal or perfect partner is not change men, but change **YOU!**

Only you. *Ever!*

You never look outside of yourself to create a change. The only change you need to create is in your thinking, perception and attitude.

Because everything you believe about yourself and men will always be reflected back to you in the men you meet. It's the Law and the men cannot help but show up (or not show up!) according to your command.

So be very careful:

what you wish for = what you think and believe.

You need to make sure that all your thoughts are in line with, or congruent with, what you want.

And that is your only job:

to realize that all your life and love results are created by you, by instructing your own brain to carry out your commands and turn them into your reality.

When you finally understand that nothing in your life is random and, now that you know that you are creating it all, you discover your power to stop running old programs and ideas which sabotage your creations and replace them with programs that actually serve you.

CASE STUDY

When my 53-year-old client came to me, she had never had a happy, solid relationship in her life.

She had always struggled with finding the right man. She felt bullied, abused, used and she was blaming herself, believing that there was something wrong with her to deserve that kind of treatment.

During our first session together, I helped her to figure out that her fear and dislike of men came from a deep-seated fear of her father, who had physically abused her.

That was the very moment when she had lost trust in men, and had started thinking that men would always let her down, hurt her and never protect her.

And that moment meant that all her relationships were doomed before they even got off the ground.

After she understood the reason for her failed relationships and we worked on her programming of how she thought about men, within 2 weeks she met her perfect man.

We continued working to ensure that all her thought processes were beneficial, and then she managed to build and secure the relationship of her life.

So, you see, it can be done; and much easier and faster than you think.

*You just need to find out **what** is in your way; remove that and the world is your oyster!*

This is a huge turnaround, but it is the first step to getting what you want.

So, are you ready?

Let's go for it…

CHAPTER 2

The Brief: Do You Know What You Want?

The very first step to any success is to know **EXACTLY** and **SPECIFICALLY** what you want. Otherwise known as **THE BRIEF.**

Because if you don't know what you want, how can you expect to find it?

I have to say that I have never met a client who knew exactly what they wanted. Every time I ask any of my clients or audiences what they want out of life or relationships, all I hear is a silence where you could so easily hear a penny drop.

I call it one of the worst illnesses of humankind. We have completely lost our ability to imagine what we want, know what we want…and do not get me started about knowing how to get it or at least making the very first step!

And yet, the ability to imagine is the most important ability in anyone's life.

Did you know that **you can have absolutely anything you can imagine?**

And that whatever you can imagine is *meant* to be and for you to have?

Well, in that case, wouldn't it be wonderful and beneficial to learn how to set goals, imagine them and figure out how to make them happen?

So, I bet that, from early childhood, you have been imagining how you will get married, have a family and live happy ever after. And you did it right. Because life is a fairy tale…

Children get it right each and every time, because they spend their whole lives imagining things. Which is the *only* way that leads to happiness and getting what you want.

They can imagine so easily and effortlessly because the poor, unbeneficial programming has not kicked in yet. They see life as it should be and as it – indeed – could be. It is we, the adults, who spoil it for them by our own wrong beliefs and perceptions.

Be more like kids!! They understand fairy tales and their true meaning…you can have the princess or the prince, you just need to make an effort, not give up and keep going until she or he says YES!!

Our imagination can create 1000 times better and more powerful stories than any Hollywood movie.

That is why I always get annoyed at people saying "it is just a movie; these things do not happen in real life". That is **so not true**. Far more amazing things and miracles happen every day to millions of people.

So, coming back to the love of your life, your **SP (*Specific* or *Special Person*)**; it can be your ex, it could be your crush or someone you have not met yet, your ideal partner – do you know everything about him?

If not, then start thinking...

I make my clients write whole lists of what their perfect partner should look like and be like.

And I always add: whatever you miss and don't write down, you most likely will not get, so do a brilliant job and think it through until you have nothing more to add.

Because if you don't actively decide what you want, you will continue to operate in default mode and blame what shows up on a malicious Universe or a shortage of decent men!

There is a huge difference between saying "I want someone lovely, kind and sexy" - those are only 3 qualities - **and designing the love of your life;** I am thinking more along the lines of 300 qualities you should be writing down.

Because guess what? Your results, literally, depend on how specific you are.

Part of us wants to believe that it is random. When asked what we want, we can't specify, except in terms of the previous experiences – so we know what we don't want; we don't want someone who is lazy or disrespectful or unkind.

However, when it comes to describing what we do want, we either don't believe we can have it, or we sit back and expect the Universe to delight us - then expect that our handsome prince will just appear, recognize how wonderful we are and sweep us off our feet.

Then, when the handsome prince turns out to be less than a match for our specifications, we wonder why!

It's easy to blame it on fate or on men… they are all the same, they always cheat, lie, let you down…whatever!

But that's not it! It is **your** CHOICE. You get to choose…how amazing is that?

Literally, it is like going to a supermarket and picking anything you fancy: ice cream, oranges, strawberries, caviar, Prosecco, prosciutto, flowers, magazines, pancakes, chocolate, salmon, gnocchi, watermelon, dates, basil, mint, nuts… just anything you fancy.

If you can do that with your shopping, why can't you do it with the love of your life?

And now I am telling you – you CAN!!

It is exactly like telling your family you want a big, white handbag for Christmas. And then receiving one made from fake leather which you know will disintegrate in two months because it only cost 10 dollars.

While you really meant to say "I want the new genuine leather Gucci which I will love, cherish and be proud of for a lifetime."

Or the same with a car. You say, "I want a red car."

And a SMART shows up in front of your door.

While you really meant to say "I want a red, vintage Lamborghini, year 1971, with black leather interior and red stitching".

But your brief was so vague that you got a *budget* SMART. But it's no use complaining now – after all, you did get exactly what you asked for: a red car!

See my point?

But here's the good news: this is fun!! Picking things you want is always the best fun ever. So enjoy it!!

Because the universe awaits your command - remember?

So, first you need to look inward.

Now you are aware that you have been putting up with the default mode for most of your life so far. In fact, you have been manifesting all along, but unconsciously manifesting from all the beliefs you hold about you and about men.

And now it is time to know exactly who your ideal partner is before you meet him:

What matters to you?

What are the features and characteristics of your SP that you cannot live without.

What are the musts?

And be brutally honest. This is no time for being 'a nice little girl' who has to please others by doing what *they* would like her to do.

This, my friend, is solely about **you**:

what **you** want, what **you** fancy, what **you** need.

Because guess what? – **you** do matter.

There is no one in your life who matters more than you. Therefore, do a good job! Not for anyone else. For you!!

Now we get down to the nitty-gritty, but this is such a joyful experience! Who would not *love* to *design* the love of their life?

Is it worth an hour or so of your time to start consciously manifesting what you want?

There is some work to be done.

What do you want?

Write it down. And be specific.

EXERCISE:
THE LOVE OF YOUR LIFE BLUEPRINT

Take a moment to recognise how good you are at manifesting.

Have a quick look at all those negative beliefs you held about yourself and about men, and then notice how the men in your life obediently reflected those back to you!

It doesn't matter if you *change the man*, the next man will be obliged to reflect your beliefs until you **change your beliefs!**

You were brilliant at creating by default, so now you are you ready to:

Create the man of your dreams by design.

Pick a comfortable spot in your house where you won't be disturbed. Grab a big notebook (better than a laptop – there is magic in writing – spelling it out – magic spells!) and a pen, and your favourite hot or cold drink- and start designing the love of your life.

Have a brief look back at the beliefs you held about you and about men (above); the beliefs that created what you didn't want. That's what you don't want – and it's a great starting point for you to turn it around and consciously choose what you DO want.

Now: **Re-write those beliefs as you want them to be** (Remember: Your word is your command. This is how it will be in your reality, your kingdom)

Now that you know what you do want and you know you can have anything you choose, start designing your SP, the love of your life.

Here are some guidelines to prompt you:

His Values:

For more details see The Brief in Chapter 6.

- His manners, courtesy – does he pay for dinner?
- His appearance – go for it!
- How important is family to him?
- Does he want children?
- Does he like pets?
- Does he live near you?
- Does he love to travel?
- Is he interested in politics - if so, what flavour?
- Does he like sports, the outdoors, books
- How much time does he spend with his friends?
- Does he prefer spending time with you?
- Is he happy for you to go off on your own for a couple of days, a week or so?

CASE STUDY

This is quite a funny story...

I was working with one of my clients on the list of 300 things she wanted to manifest in her new SP or ideal partner.

She was very inventive and I loved her work.

But one day she shared with me that it was not as good as it could be in the bedroom department.

I asked her whether she had put that request on her list.

She had a look and it was not there!

After I asked her to write it down and amend the list, things completely turned around for her.

This is a perfect example of what happens when you do not write down everything you want.

Because what you don't ask for, you don't get!

And when you are done with the list of everything you want in your ideal man, read it once more and put it away. No need to read it every day. You did everything you needed to do, you did well and now have the luxury of leaving it alone.

In the meantime, let's move on to other things you need to understand.

CHAPTER 3

You Are The Operant Power –
Your Thoughts Create

Your WORD is your command!

You must be a winner to get the man of your dreams.

You are in charge of your life.

You say what you want and you create it.

Your thoughts create your reality.

All your results; in love, relationships, finance, health, looks, business, career, parenting, are created by your **WORDS** and **THOUGHTS**…

Now breathe…

I know it may be a shock, but that is how it is. That is the miracle of creation right there, all backed by neuroscience and quantum physics.

See, it is not that life is happening **to** you and that there is nothing you can do about it.

You are not a victim!!

If you want the love of your life, millions in the bank, a great business, you need to **become a winner!!**

And winners create their lives and results...

You don't like your relationships?

You don't like your body?

You don't like your health?

You don't like your business?

You hate not having enough money or the money you want?

You created it all...by your thoughts, by your programming, by your mindset.

But guess what? If you created it you can re-create it, and this time properly, the way you really want it.

Your words create your reality.

If you say "I am fat", you give an instruction to your body to make you fat.

If you say "I have no money", you will create more of "not having money".

So, what really has to happen is that you start choosing and insisting on using words which get you closer to your goals.

Your thoughts dictate how **everyone** in your life treats you.

Sit with that for a few moments.

Now, consider how your beliefs (beliefs are just thoughts you *keep* thinking) have created your relationships - or lack of them - up to now.

When you realize the connection, you will see that it is vital to start being **AWARE** of your thoughts and catch them constantly, so that you can **choose** which thoughts serve your conscious intention.

Just start *noticing* what you think and start converting your thoughts from unhelpful to helpful.

And you can do that through:

1. Affirmations
2. Mental diet

Example:

Negative thinking: Men always hurt me.

Positive thinking: Men adore me, love me and respect me.

Negative thinking: Men are only after sex.

Positive thinking: Men appreciate me as a lovely person and love spending time with me.

Negative thinking: Men are not easily available.

Positive thinking: Great men are easy to find.

Best practice of affirmations:

- 3 times in one day: morning, lunch and evening
- for about 5-10 minutes each time
- spoken **out loud**
- while pacing around the room or walking outside, if possible

So, **affirmations** can easily be scheduled into your day.

However, the **mental diet** is executed every single time you hear yourself think or say something that is unbeneficial and goes against you accomplishing your goals.

The **mental diet** is the action of catching and cutting out any thought which does not serve you.

That means, for instance, in the car, while cooking, while watching TV, at work, while taking a shower, simply anytime and anywhere.

Act immediately: take the opportunity to instantly correct your thought and say the exact opposite of it, just like in the affirmations examples (but don't walk around if driving the car!)

CASE STUDY

I have had so many clients who, when they first come to me, were in unhappy relationships.

And all of them shared the same thing in common:

They believed that men always hurt them.

They never knew, until they met me, that what they believed men to be, was manifesting men to show up like that in their reality.

One particular client had a repeating pattern of every man leaving her for a younger woman, even though she was quite young herself.

So, one of our first sessions was about finding out why that was happening.

We figured out that her self-concept was poor and that she had a fear of being abandoned, which came from her early childhood when her parents divorced and her father left her.

Once we resolved that issue and she affirmed that she is safe and secure and all men treat her with respect, and that she only creates happy and long-lasting relationships, everything changed.

Now she is planning her first baby with the love of her life!

And that is exactly how it works...it is **not** what the men do, it is what ***you believe*** they will do...

CHAPTER 4

The Missing Piece

Self-love – the secret ingredient

I am sure you have heard this before…

In order for someone else to love you, you have to love yourself first!!

Every time I used to hear that, I cringed inside, because I thought "What the hell do you mean by that?

I do love myself; I don't hurt myself, I take care of myself, I do my best to look attractive, I constantly educate myself, I eat home-cooked meals…that hardly sounds like someone who does not like themself!"

The thing that I almost never heard anyone explain properly was what "loving yourself" means.

This is my version of self-love:

- I believe that self-love means rewiring your brain.
- Refusing to put up with anything but greatness.

- No longer being surrounded by toxic people and circumstances, but aiming higher; insisting on great standards.
- Constantly raising the bar.
- Refusing to be anything else but happy.
- Expecting to be treated with the utmost respect by everyone.
- Having a great zest for life.
- Loving being alive.
- Insisting on great health and looking the way you want to look.
- Refusing to "give into" ageing (because that, too, is a choice).
- Studying every day of your life: life-long learning
- Improving constantly.
- Thinking kindly of yourself.
- Being positive, happy and not getting involved in dramas.
- Picking the thoughts which are beneficial to you.
- **And, most of all, consciously making all the decisions which lead me to happiness, great health, all the money I want, the body I want, the relationships I want, the business I want.**

Simply picking thoughts and making decisions which get me to my desires and goals in the fastest, happiest and most fun way ever.

So, if I asked you now "What do you love about yourself?", how many words would you respond with?

Five, ten, twenty?

Because that is usually what happens when I ask my clients to write down what they love about themselves.

The average number of things they love about themselves is 12.

And the most common sentence I hear before they do that is:

"It would be easier to tell you what I *hate* about myself".

It is incredibly sad and worrying.

So, the last time I asked my client to list the things he loved about himself, I did a test. I wanted to see how well I am doing.

And so, in the same time that he wrote 12 things, I wrote 138 things. The first time I ever did it, I wrote 40.

And here is the shocker:

The more loving things you can write about yourself, the better your life gets.

The more money you make. The better partner you get. The better business gets. Generally, the better success you enjoy.

Because your results, in any sphere of life, are dependent on your self-love.

The comments from other people, deductions you make about your attractiveness, worthiness, right to choose, importance, all your negative beliefs which you *think* have come from others, are only the result of others reflecting back what **you** believe about ***yourself***.

The amazing truth is that you can decide what to think and, therefore, you get to decide how others treat you!

If you get that, why would you ***ever*** say anything negative about yourself again?!

So, **stop it now!** Stop judging yourself. Stop the negative self-talk of, "I am fat", "I'm stupid", I'm too old", whatever. If you want to change something, do that. In the meantime, embrace it, for if you reject it and judge it to be 'bad', others cannot help but mirror that back to you.

EXERCISE:

So, I have a little exercise for you to do:

Take a pen and paper and write down a list of **50 things** you love about yourself, and do not give up until you get them down on paper.

And when you are done, I want you to continue, to make it a grand total of **100 things** you love about yourself.

And watch what happens…you will see your life change in front of your eyes.

CHAPTER 5

Create The Best Version Of You!

I ALWAYS STRIVE TO BE THE BEST VERSION OF MYSELF

Because the better I get, the better my results.

Who are you now?

Let me guess:

- you may lack self-confidence
- you could love yourself more
- you lack trust in men or maybe in people in general
- you were hurt quite a bit in the past and that makes you afraid
- you always hope for the best, yet your results are not that brilliant
- you know you deserve love but it is just not happening, or you even believe (consciously or subconsciously) that you do not deserve love
- you think that you always end up being hurt

- you are impatient
- it is difficult for you to have faith
- you give up all too easily
- you self-sabotage just so that no one can hurt you
- you push people away just so they cannot hurt you
- you are frustrated and sad because time is ticking away and not much is happening

I am sure that you will tick at least some of these. Some of you will tick almost all the boxes. And it is the most common thing. All my clients are like that before they come to me.

But have you ever wondered who you would really like to be?

You keep looking at that picture of Marilyn Monroe and wish to be as sexy and attractive. Or Audrey Hepburn, wishing to be as classy. Or Betty White, wishing to be as funny.

Guess what? You can be all of that. Because your personality is your choice.

You *say* who you want to be.

(Remember: your wish is, literally, your command!)

It has nothing to do with your genes and DNA.

Remember; you are in charge. Completely and utterly.

You want to be confident?
You want to be attractive?

You want to be relaxed?

You want to be fun?

You want to be sexy?

Well, be that!!

Notice that is not about you being 'wrong' or not good enough, but about you being in alignment with the 'you' you choose to present to the world. This will be the version of 'you' that you will see reflected back at you from others, so it makes sense to create the best version of 'you' that you can imagine -

Just because you can!

EXERCISE:

So, take a pen and paper and start writing down all about the person you want to be.

And when you are finished, do the same as you have done with your ideal partner list:

Put it away, forget it and affirm:

> I am self-confident.
> I am gorgeous.
> Men love me.
> I am a great manifestor.
> I am successful.
> I always get what I want.
> I am super productive.
> I am very creative.
> I am adorable.
> I am love.
> I am lovable.
> I am loving.
> And everything else you want to be.

And keep adding every time you have a new thought and until you have nothing more to add...

CHAPTER 6

───── ⟡ ─────

How To Manifest: The Rules, The Entire Step-By-Step Process

HOW MANIFESTING WORKS

M anifesting is just wonderful.

I so wish everyone in the world knew how to manifest.

There would be a lot of very happy and fulfilled people

and most of the negative things we are experiencing nowadays would disappear by default.

Why I love manifesting most is not actually getting what I want, now within seconds, it is that it has calmed me down, and given me the peace and assurance of *knowing* that everything I want, I already have.

And it has taught me to be the person I have always wanted to be but didn't know how to become.

Because manifesting is all about:

- Being patient
- Ignoring circumstances
- Ignoring time
- Not reacting emotionally
- Knowing that I can have anything I want
- Having everything available to me
- Having faith in myself, the world and other people
- Knowing I deserve everything I want
- Being responsible for all my results
- Not blaming anyone else for my life
- Having superpowers to change everything in my life
- Creating everything I have ever wanted through the power of my mind

And you have to admit, that sounds pretty good, not to mention miraculous!!

Manifesting is a Success System backed by Science

Manifesting is not some random theory, but a scientific process derived from the principles of Quantum Physics - how this world works -and neuroscience - how the brain works.

The theory supports it, but, more to the point, it works in practice.

The bottom line is this:

Anything you think and believe, you get!!

Whatever you imprint on your subconscious mind, the subconscious mind then projects to the outer world, and it has to happen. It's the law.

- You imprinted it on your subconscious mind
- Your subconscious mind projects that in the outer world
- The outer world has to bring that into reality

Your subconscious mind runs 95% of your life - your conscious mind runs only 5% of your life.

So, whatever is in your subconscious mind, happens by default.

You get whatever is running in your programming and call it fate! But all it takes to start running by your conscious choice-your design - is to **pay attention**! That is why it is so important to work with it all the time.

The importance of PAYING ATTENTION...

You may have heard people say "Oh, manifesting can't be as simple as just focusing on something and it appears!" It is, but **there is a price to pay**. The price of **paying** attention is ongoing. You can't just let up and expect everything to stay on course.

It is important to keep correcting your thoughts and uncovering what beliefs you have about money, love, weight, health, about anything…people, politics, the outside world.

You need to keep correcting the thoughts and beliefs into the state of love, into the best state there is, the most positive state there is. Love is Attention and Attention is Love.

When you do that, by the law of physics, whatever you give out you get back multiplied.

All manifesting is also about knowing exactly and specifically what you want, imagining it through something we call an "end scene" and leaving it alone until we can physically see it in our lives.

And it's about following several important rules to ensure that we get what we want easily, effortlessly and fast.

So, let's get into it!!

Manifesting works really easily.

The main thing you have to understand is that manifesting is totally natural, and it is something we are doing all the time.

We have been doing it from the time we were born; we just did not call it manifestation, we called it "stuff happens".

It is a process whereby you think something, and that 'thing' becomes real.

- Your beliefs and your thoughts become real.
- So, what you really want to do is to have **great** beliefs and thoughts!
- For the better your thoughts, the better your quality of life.

So, manifesting is natural. It is easy. And you have always been doing it.

The only thing we are doing differently in this book, is that we are doing it consciously.

This means we are increasing the success rate of your manifestations and we are learning to do it in a, basically, bullet-proof style.

Anyone can do it all the time perfectly… it is easy!

There are so many coaches that I watch and follow. They make manifesting sound like there are thousands of rules, it is very time consuming and it feels like a chore…like boot camp!

I want to make it really easy…because it is.

I know everything about the process but, in summary, if you skip all the 'stuff' and you learn just what you need to learn -and you always go back to it – you will win.

So, here is a quick checklist with all you need to **get started now.**

Manifesting – so what do I need to do…?

1. THE BRIEF - KNOW EXACTLY AND SPECIFICALLY WHAT YOU WANT

The very first thing to do in the manifesting process is to create the perfect brief of what you want.

You basically have to find out very specifically what you want.

For example, if you want a coffee, you need to ask yourself:

- is it an iced coffee?
- is it a latte?
- is it a large one?
- is it a small one?

You need to say exactly, and very specifically, what you want.

If you were to go to the counter and ask for 'a coffee' they would not be able to serve you as there are so many types of coffees, they would not know what you wanted.

So, be very precise - "I want a one-shot latte and could you put a little bit more milk in it, thank you".

Manifesting your SP/the love of your life

You need to know exactly who you want to be your partner or husband.

You need to write the list of 300 things you want your ideal partner to have.

Example:

- He is tall
- He has gorgeous dark hair
- He brings me breakfast in bed
- He always puts dirty clothes in the basket, not next to it
- He has a great sense of humour
- He loves wearing a beautiful cologne
- He dresses well
- He deals with my car insurance
- He washes the dishes
- He always remembers to take out the bins
- He loves cuddling
- He loves the same movies as me
- He loves classical music
- His favourites are Mozart and Bach
- He takes me out dancing
- He adores Thai food
- He loves Dijon mustard
- He is very considerate
- He is very polite…

See, it is not that difficult.

You can do it.

And remember, you may not get what you do not write down, so do your best!!

After you have decided very specifically what you want, you then create the end scene:

The car is a great example because everyone can imagine it. Just change the make and model to make it real for you. Refer to this checklist often, learning to replace the car with a house or a lover or anything you choose to experience.

You want a car?

Well, you could get a Skoda.

So, if you want a car, you need to say "I want last year's orange Lamborghini and I want the seats in beige upholstery."

When you know exactly what you want, then you create your end scene.

Creating your end scene is such fun because it is something that makes you happy. I mean, who wouldn't enjoy designing exactly what they want to show up in their life?!

2. THE END SCENE

The second thing you need to do in manifesting is to create the end scene, also known as the imaginal act.

So, let's say you imagine already having the Lamborghini; the color…the model…the year of the car.

Spend 5-10 seconds **imagining** it through your own eyes in the 'first person' view (that is- experiencing it first hand from your perspective, not observing yourself from the outside.)

You are sitting in the car…you are touching it…you are feeling it…your hands are on the wheel.

How do you feel, knowing that you already have this car?

"Wow this is amazing…what does this button do? This is excellent…I feel so happy…this is so exciting; I can't wait to drive this car."

Do this many times and for many days until it feels absolutely real!

After you have had fun with it – abandon it and **leave it alone**. Just go about your business: cooking, dancing, horse riding etc.

Try not to think about it.

RULES FOR CREATING AN END-SCENE

- Imagine it for only 5-10 seconds
- Imagine that your desire has already happened
- Do it in the first-person view
- Feel it real, do it very vividly – know what you are wearing, what perfume you are wearing, what your hair looks like, what your body looks like, what the cup looks like, where you are sitting.
- You need to keep doing that until you are very happy with the scene, until you are satisfied, and you know you have done it

That means you have created it in the end scene.

Therefore, it already exists!

You have finished your manifestation at the time you have completed your end scene.

It already exists somewhere else and you just need to let the Universe/Higher Power/Source deliver it to you.

3. CREATION IS DONE

So, the second you have finished your end scene, you have created your manifestation.

Manifestation is not created when it arrives to you.

It is created when you do your end scene.

Hence it already exists and the creation is done!!

Your creation is done/finished and you have done your work. There is nothing to worry about - it is already yours!

So: Congratulations!!

Now it has to come to pass in your physical reality:

- — If you have done your end scene properly
- — And if you keep up with all the rules mentioned in this book...

4. PARALLEL REALITIES

The concept of parallel realities is so amazing!

From your school days you are aware that the Universe is infinite; it doesn't start, and it doesn't end.

Everything in this world is infinite.

The number of possibilities you have are infinite.

Example:

It is not just that you can go to Tesco or go to Waitrose (or Walmart in the US) to do your food shopping. No. You have an infinite number of opportunities. You can go to ALL the supermarkets, or you can order it online or you can simply grow things in your garden. You can do whatever you want.

You have SO many choices.

So, there are an infinite number of parallel realities.

Your brain sees time in a linear and continuous way. You do not see snapshots.

Your brain sees continuous time.

Imagine a movie, it is made up of thousands of little windows all joined to make the movie. THAT is what time looks like.

Time is this '...one window, one window, one window, one window...' an infinite number of windows per second. And each of these windows is a parallel reality.

So, while I am talking to you, I have an infinite amount of choices I can pick - I can do whatever I want: go make a drink, eat an ice cream, go running etc. I can do anything I want and not one 'snapshot' is the same as another 'snapshot'.

If I were to scan your body, your body does not stay the same.

Your body would not just be different every day, but in every minute and every second!

The levels of serotonin, oxytocin and insulin in your body will be different in every second of your life. Your body changes several times a second.

That is how parallel realities work. There is an infinite number of parallel realities and **you just pick** the ones you like.

It is a one big quantum supermarket...

Example:

You go into the quantum supermarket with your shopping list and you select the things you want: steak and chips, ice cream, a house in Nice, a swimming pool, a Lamborghini...

Whatever you can imagine, you can have!

How does this relate to your creation?

When you create your end scene, your imaginal act, it is created, and it exists in one of those parallel realities you choose from.

And it is your job to stay focused on it to get it.

You must keep checking your mental diet making sure you think the right thoughts and the right beliefs.

You pick that reality that you want but, similarly, you can pick any other reality.

Example:

You do not manifest your SP because you have negative beliefs about love or poor relationships.

It is your job to make sure that what you think about today is far better than what you thought yesterday, last week, or this time last year.

Another very important thing about parallel realities is this:

You live in your 3D reality or reality as we know it…

But when you created your end scene, you created your desire in a different parallel reality.

And to manifest your desire physically in your 3D reality, your 3D and the other parallel reality have to merge.

And that is the time lag between you already having what you want in your end scene and that desire coming to pass in your 3D world.

5. LET IT GO

So, you created your exact brief.

Then you created your end scene.

Your creation is done and it already exists.

Now you have a really important goal ahead of you:

Letting go…

This is one of the most difficult things to do in manifesting.

People are really so hung up on what they want and they do not want to let go.

Letting go means "I know I have manifested it… I know it exists…I know there is a parallel reality where I am super healthy or very rich or have my SP".

And, by **letting go, I mean:**

- – I am not worried,
- – I am not obsessed,
- – I don't care,
- – I am not thinking about it every 3 seconds.
- – I am living my life the way I would live my life *if* I were already super healthy, or very rich or with my SP. Because I already have all of the above, remember?

So…you are letting go of what you want?

Are you letting go of your desire?

No! On the contrary; you made it very obvious and very clear to yourself, your subconscious mind and to the Universe, *exactly* what you want.

IT IS NOT FORGOTTEN!!!

But you do need to stop *stressing* about it and stop thinking about it.

You need to stop asking:

"Where is it? How is it going to happen?"

You need to completely stop thinking about it, which takes effort (I will teach you how to do that).

And you just drop it. Do not notice it, do not think about it, do not talk about it.

Most of all, you do not talk to your family and friends about it as they may tell you "you are crazy".

Just figure out what you want, do your end scene and then drop it. Do not think about it again.

And if you do, then go back to your end scene.

Every time you have doubts, fears, you are desperate and needy or you really, really, really, want it to happen – all this is doing is **DELAYING IT!**

There are two parameters you cannot control in conscious manifesting; they are **Time** and **How it will happen**. They are not your problem.

The fastest way you can manifest is to **NOT** think about it.

But, of course, if it has to do with bad health issues, your specific person, or how to pay your rent, it can be very difficult not to think about it as, obviously, you are very worried. I completely get that.

But you have to let go of that.

Remember, the more you try to control *when* it happens and *how* it happens the longer it will take for the manifestation to come to pass in your 3D reality…

The greatest things always happen when we don't *need* them to happen.

So, the fastest way to manifest is:

- End scene
- It is done!!
- It already exists…
- ***OVER!***

6. THE BRIDGE OF INCIDENTS

So, by now, I'm sure all of you know that to manifest you need to do those 3 things:

1. You need to know what you want, very, very specifically.

So, you want your SP to be kind to you, to be nice, to be sexy, to be romantic, to take you out for dinner, to be lovely and treat you well. You want him to always support you and always be there for you and you want him to take you to Rome and Venice and Santa Fe.

Mostly, you want to be married to him with three children.

2. You make an end scene about it.

So, let's say your end scene is of driving a car, sun roof down, three babies in the back, sitting next to him. Your hand, bearing your wedding ring, rests on his lap. And he says, "Hello Mrs. Wright".

Use his surname (you must have taken his surname when you married him). So, he says, "Hello Mrs. Wright, how are you today?"

And then you say, "Hello Mr. Wright, I'm so happy!" and he says, "I love you", and that's your end scene, because it says:

- You are extremely happy
- You're married because there's a wedding ring on your finger

- He called you by his surname, not your maiden name
- There are three children and it's lovely and you're super happy and he couldn't be happier and he knows he loves you.

So, that's it.

- You play that scene for 5-10 seconds.
- You can loop it around and repeat 2 or 3 times.
- You see it through your own first-person experience.
- You smell it, touch it, feel it. It's very vivid.
- You play it so often in your mind until you believe that it's done, you created it, you manifested it already in another parallel reality.

3. You let go.

You stop being desperate and needy, and you stop controlling how your manifestation happens and when.

We have already spoken about how your manifestation is **already done**, and all that is left is for you to let it go and leave it alone!

So, what happens in between creating your end scene and it coming into your reality?

I refer to this as: **The Bridge of Incidents**

What does that mean?

It means that lots of things have to happen in order for that to come into your reality.

Many, many things.

So, let's say the love of your life is married. In order to marry you, he'll need to sort out his situation. He needs to pretty much legally divorce first.

If you're in different countries, he needs to either move to your country or you need to move to his country.

Lots of things – *incidents* - have to take place in order for you to get what you want.

And some of those things will be lovely and some of those things could be absolutely nasty, but you need to ignore that.

Just know that everything you've done is **your part.**

You have **completed** your work, so **you're 100% guaranteed to get what you want** and whatever happens in the middle is none of your business.

Everything happens for a reason, good or bad, and **everything is leading you to what you want.**

So, you do not react emotionally to any of that, just observe what's going on and say, "Everything's happening for a reason."

Everything is working in my favor and everything that happens leads me to what I want, whether it's good or bad, that's not up to me, either can happen.

I'm not going to judge it. I'm just going to take it as a test because I know that 100% of the time, whatever happens works in my favor."

And that's all.

Remember the end scene where you and your SP are driving along in the car as Mr. and Mrs. Wright, with your three babies in the back seat?

Let's look at the bridge of incidents that might occur between imagining your end scene and it coming into your reality.

In order for your SP to divorce - and let's say he is relatively rich – he needs a reason to divorce, so maybe the wife will be a pain or have an affair, who knows. Maybe his children will be annoying, or maybe he'll realize his self-value or maybe something will happen and his wife and children will move to New York and maybe she will find someone else.

Anything can happen, **it's none of your business.**

Imagine how many things have to happen in order for him to divorce, split properties, say "goodbye" to the family and buy a new house or invite you over, or move to your place, all of that; that takes a lot of effort, all that is a bridge of incidents.

And, whatever happens, you have to take it and say,

"Yep, working for me, it's always working for me. I know that."

And that's how you manifest in the fastest possible way!!

EXERCISE:
'PRACTICE BEFORE SLEEPING'

First, think about what your scene will look like, then take a pen and paper and:

    (i) Write down in the smallest detail your whole imaginal scene,

   (ii) Then start imagining it until you get the script just as you want it.

  (iii) Then visualize it in a relaxed state for 5-10 seconds. This works best if practiced in the last couple of minutes before falling asleep. You can either 'self-hypnotize' by looking upwards into your eyelids until your eyes close, or breathe deeply and close your eyes, then start visualizing. Allow yourself to imagine it, looping the scene around in your mind several times until you fall asleep.

---

7. NOT REACTING EMOTIONALLY TO THE 3D WORLD

Now I would love to talk to you about our **3D world...**

The 3D world means the reality we live in, everything around you: the sky, your TV, magazines, hairdryer, mobile phone, people, job, colleagues, pizza you are eating while reading this book.

It certainly seems very real, however it is just our perception.

It doesn't really exist by the laws of quantum physics.

We create reality through either "I see this" or "I don't see that" or "I think this" or "I don't think that".

So, things happen in our 'so called' reality, our normal life.

We talked about the bridge of incidents and the 2 steps you need to perform to get what you want:

- You decide specifically what you want
- You create the end scene

And the bridge of incidents just means the time that passes between where you're at right now and that point where you are already married, possibly already have children, happy ever after - your end scene.

And to connect your specific brief and your happy ending is the bridge of incidents.

Things have to happen.

There are lots of people and lots of things that have to shift in order for you to get what you want.

I explained that by using the example of going to the supermarket, and buying coffee. Lots of people have to do lots of things like make your seat free, allow you to park easily, boil some water, push a button to pour your coffee, be a cashier and take the money from you, etc.

That takes a lot of people to get you ONE coffee.

And now imagine how many people have to be shifted in order for you to get your SP (specific person, ideal partner) back or find a new one.

The thing is, almost no one tells you what the bridge of incidents can look like. It can come as a shock to you, that's why I wanted to explain it properly now, so you don't feel too surprised later.

Because the things which can happen in the bridge of incidents can be lovely but also quite unpleasant.

So you've done your end scene, and a week later your SP texts you:

"I never want to see you again."

And all you have to do is say, "OK, I understand".

However, you keep thinking "No, No, No, No, No! You are already with me; we are already married"

"I'm not buying that, because I've manifested you, you're already with me. We already live together and have babies and are married in our parallel reality.

So, you can tell me whatever you want, but I know the truth is different."

That's how we deal with things which, seemingly, go 'wrong'...**we do not react EMOTIONALLY!!**

Let's say that your SP has a third party or they start dating.

It could happen - and you manifested that, by the way!

You see them on social media, and you react, "Oh God! Now what do I do? It's over!".

No.

You just laugh at it and you say, "No, you're already living with me and we already have three babies".

The end scene is your only true, real reality. You need to stay in that end scene and know that you two are already together, regardless of what you see in your 3D world.

You need to have unwavering faith, or, better than that, a knowing; knowing is better than faith.

When you convince your brain and yourself that you know this, there's no power in this world which can prevent you from having it.

So, we never react emotionally to circumstances or to whatever 3D world - our reality - shows us, because it is always working out in our favour every single time.

You have to hold on to that belief and just relax and laugh and say "well that was hilarious but I know better."

I hope that makes sense...

Jana Tip: Anytime you feel sad and ask, 'Where is it?'

- Go back and revisit your end scene
- You cannot be sad about something you already have

Much of the 'reality' you are experiencing right now is the result of thoughts you held weeks or even months ago. Then again, it is possible to just think of an old friend then receive a call from them immediately.

So, do everything you can to pick and stay in the parallel reality you just created by using your end scene.

8. LIVING FROM THE END

So, you did your end scene. Great.

What follows after doing your end scene is:

- Noticing your contradictory thoughts (contradictory to what your goal is, such as "men are horrible", "I cannot find a decent man")
- Doing your affirmations
- Following your mental diet
- Ignoring circumstances
- Not reacting emotionally
- Disregarding time
- Not being needy
- And mainly **LIVING IN THE END…**

And I will explain to you right now **what living in the end means…**

It is an unwavering knowing that you are already married to your ideal partner, you are happy, you have a wonderful happy long term loyal relationship and you have it right now.

Because, as we said, by visualizing the end scene, you already created it.

So, the easiest and fastest way to get your ideal SP in the 3D reality is to live as if you are already together.

No, you do not have to set the dinner table for two. Nothing like that.

You simply assume that you are right now with the love of your life and that is that.

You are not waiting for them to show up, you do not need them to text you, you don't need them to call you, you don't need them to ask you out, because if you are married to them already, you definitely would not be waiting for any of those things.

Because you are already together!

Find the Love of Your Life in 30 Days!

9. HOW TO TRUST IN MANIFESTING

In order for you to have a complete and unwavering trust in manifesting, let's do some practice which will prove to you beyond any doubt that this works.

EXERCISE:

Write down 10 things every day you want to manifest, for at least 30 days, and at the end of every week, tick all things which manifested.

Buy a fresh notebook and, every evening before you go to bed write, down what you would like to happen.

Examples:

- See a butterfly
- See an orange Lamborghini
- Get a free coffee
- Be offered chocolate cake
- Receive an unexpected present
- A neighbour smiles at you
- A stranger offers to help you
- You hear from someone you haven't heard from in years
- See a picture with a giraffe
- Hear an ABBA song

And then start paying attention to your life; to the things you see and hear and, the next day, or once a week, go and tick off everything from the list which actually happened.

You may be very surprised how easily this works.

Go for it!!

---

10. BLOCKS TO MANIFESTATION

Many people find it challenging to manifest or to manifest fast enough.

And there are specific reasons for that.

They are called contradictory thoughts, negative thoughts, negative beliefs and manifesting blocks.

I will list most of them now so you can evaluate how much you have conquered up until now and what needs your attention:

- **What do I believe about manifesting?**
  - Manifesting does not work
  - It is very difficult for me to manifest, etc.

- **What do I believe about my SP?**
  - He doesn't love me
  - He never wants to get married
  - He does not want to live with me, etc.

- **What do I think my SP believes about me?**
  - He thinks I am fat
  - He thinks I am not loyal, etc.

- **What do I believe about myself?**
  - I am not attractive enough to find a man
  - I am overweight
  - I don't have enough money, etc.

- **What do I believe about love?**
  - Love is difficult to find
  - Love hurts, etc.

- **What do I believe about relationships?**
  - Relationships never work
  - I have to be submissive in all my relationships
  - No one ever appreciated me, etc.

- **What do I believe about men in general?**
  - Men cheat
  - Men are horrible
  - Men have no feelings, etc.

- **What do I believe about my life and my powers?**
  - I never win
  - Nothing ever works out for me
  - I don't know why bad things keep happening to me, etc.

And then, of course, all you need to do is turn those negative beliefs into positive beneficial ones by affirming and mental diet.

Notice: As you list **the beliefs you hold about love and relationships, for example,** keep the **positive** beliefs which serve you, and where your beliefs are **negative,** turn them into **positive** statements.

For example:

I am patient.

I have faith that I always get what I want.

I never give up.

"Men are attracted to me"

"I always get what I want in relationships."

But **negative** statements like "All men cheat." turn into **positive** statements: "Men are faithful."

Negative: "Relationships are hard work and stressful"

Turn to

Positive: "Relationships are easy and fun"

Negative: "Men are only looking for young women"

Turn to

Positive: "Men are looking for all kinds of women."

And now just keep going, collecting the positive statements for all of the previous questions until you have nothing more to add!

11. SABOTAGING BEHAVIOURS

Now, before we go any further, I would like to address some important factors that can seriously affect your manifesting results, and they are:

- neediness
- desperation
- emotional attachment
- rejection
- being excited

Neediness

Most people are just too needy for healthy, long lasting relationships.

They NEED to be loved, adored, be given attention, etc.

This occurs for one reason only: **because they are not capable of supplying those feelings and emotions to themselves.**

It is surprisingly common and it usually happens when your childhood needs were not met, so that you are looking outside of yourself to get them. That makes you dependent on anyone who has a potential to supply them to you.

And it makes for a very uneven relationship, where you are losing your personal power and you are willingly giving it to someone else.

That can never work. Ever.

The only thing you *NEED* to do is:

- be your own person
- love yourself unconditionally
- respect yourself
- stop needing attention
- stop needing other people
- stop needing the validation or approval of others
- and, most importantly, be happy on your own

Because after all, your ideal partner does not complete you, they only enhance your already happy, perfect, content life.

Desperation

Most clients I meet are desperate to be with someone.

They are desperate to have a relationship.

And the first thing I say is "You need to stop that!"

No one wants to be with a desperate person, who comes across as clingy and needy.

Men adore women who are self-confident, who know what they want and who can take care of themselves.

That is a great basis for a fantastic relationship.

Desperation will make them run a mile… and you don't want that!

So be your own person, be busy getting on with your life. Have fun and stop being so hung up on being with someone.

Then, and only then, will your Prince Charming show up.

Emotional attachment

Emotional attachment becomes a problem mainly when it comes to wanting your ex back or wanting someone you already know.

You have already created emotions with regard to them and it is highly possible those emotions act as a manifesting block.

Remember: the best place to be is 'not needing anyone'.

To do that in practice means to stay strong, to put yourself on a pedestal, to be happy with who you are and to be happy with your life.

If you cannot get to that state, I think it would benefit you greatly to speak to a coach who can help you to free yourself from the emotional attachment.

Rejection

If you were rejected by your ex or your 'friend with benefits', you may still be playing that old story in your mind.

He hurt me. It was horrible. He is mean. He should not have done that. How could he do it to me. He never loved me. He is just cruel. I loved him so much and this is how he repaid me.

Those are some of the most common thoughts people have after an unpleasant break up or heated discussion.

And if these are your thoughts, those will be your manifestations.

Because what happens when you think "he hurts me"?

He has to keep doing things which will hurt you, such as not being with you, not calling you, not talking to you, not marrying you.

You have to find the strength in you and start playing the story in your mind that you actually want:

I manifested the break up. He loves me. He misses me. He is wonderful. He always has my interests at heart. He is caring and supportive.

Just focus on the things you do want and not on the things you don't want. As easy as that.

Being excited

We all love being excited.

I get it.

But think about it. When are you excited?

When you get or achieve something what was a huge thing to get. Something you have never had or done before.

So, what does that mean? It means that every time when you get excited you are sending out signals that you are not used to having it. You are saying that receiving that thing is not expected or doesn't come naturally to you.

And our goal in this book is convincing your brain that you are already in the relationship of your dreams with the ideal partner.

So, you need to project that you already have your ideal partner, it is a done deal and it feels normal. Just as normal as breathing. Nothing special or weird about it.

That is the way to go…

12. EVERYTHING IS EASY AND NATURAL

If you work under the premise that everything in life is difficult, hard, complicated, impossible and has to be hard-earned, then it will have to be just that – for whatever you say, goes!

Do you remember how your brain has to make everything you think and say happen?

Wouldn't it be much nicer, calmer and stress-free to say:

- Everything is easy
- Everything is effortless
- Everything is possible

Every time, whenever I used to slip up and think about something being difficult, I said to myself "my life is perfect" and I instantly snapped out of it and felt amazing.

Start changing your attitude from being a victim to being a winner.

13. CURRENT CIRCUMSTANCES DO NOT MATTER

So many people believe in circumstances.

Example:

- My SP lives in another country
- My SP has a third party
- My SP said he will never live with anyone, etc.

Nothing in life is set in stone...everything is malleable!!

You need to remember that you create all circumstances with your thinking and beliefs.

And, if you know how to create circumstances, you can create new ones!

So, let's go for the beneficial ones this time around.

It does not matter what you see in 3D reality.

It is within your power to change that.

CASE STUDY

One of my clients came to me after she had broken up with her boyfriend.

The break up was bad enough but it got even worse.

In one month, she found out that he had a "3rd party".

It was his ex-girlfriend.

My client was, understandably, devastated.

Yet again, I had to explain to someone that she had manifested the break up, and that she had manifested the 3rd party by her own insecurity which stemmed from her poor self-concept and fear of being abandoned.

We worked on not noticing the 3rd party, putting herself first, believing she is the best person for him: and she got back with him in less than one month after our session!

Apparently, he asked her out and he brought her flowers.

Anything is possible when you believe it is!!

14. COMPETITION DOES NOT MATTER

Have you noticed how competition never matters to self-confident people?

Self-confident people just know they can have anything they want and they go about life with ease, grace and effortlessness…they behave very naturally.

They know they are the best available option and their belief is exactly what helps them manifest anything they want.

So, be self-confident, have great self-esteem (esteem yourself!), know you can have anything you want and stop paying attention to competition.

Only ever pay attention to you.

After all, you created the competition and now you can create 'no competition'!

And all you need to do is to stop paying attention to it.

Because anything we stop giving attention to has to cease existing.

That is the law!!

15. TIME DOES NOT MATTER

So let me guess…

You want your results *right now*.

You keep wondering where is he; where is the love of my life?

And that fact alone is a block to your manifestation.

Time does not exist.

It is a social construct.

In manifesting, we have to disregard time.

The second you finished your end scene, you have, literally, created what you want, just in a different parallel reality.

Hence you have nothing to wait for. It is done!!!

The only thing which has to happen now – unless your negative beliefs are in the way and you have to remove them – is for that parallel reality to catch up with 3D.

That is all there is to it.

It will always take time and also depend on how many people have to be shifted and how many events have to happen in order for you to get what you want.

So, the more you fret about the time, the more time between you and the physical manifestation you will manifest.

Just leave the time out of it; **you do not control** how long anything takes, so just let go of trying to.

And that, my friends, is the fastest way to get exactly what you want!!

16. FEARS AND DOUBTS

We all have fears and doubts.

But here's the thing. Manifesting is about having unwavering faith, belief, knowing that what you want is coming, no matter what.

So, your job, in the meantime, is to shift your doubts and beliefs and make yourself completely trust that what you want is yours already, and nothing and no one can take it away from you - **except:**

YOU, your negative beliefs, fears and doubts.

17. GRATITUDE

What am I grateful for?

And, to conclude this chapter, I have a wonderful exercise ready for you.

Take a pen and paper and write 100+ things you are grateful for.

You are wondering "Why?", I am sure.

Because the state of gratitude changes your brain, makes you happier, makes you calmer, and greatly increases your openness to receiving more wonderful things.

Because we can never have that which we do not appreciate.

I can assure you that, if you do it well, you will be able to find hundreds of thousands of things to be grateful for.

The last time I did this exercise, I wrote down 648 things in 30 minutes.

Example:

- Health
- Looks
- Cats
- Car
- Petrol
- House

- Nails
- Eyes
- Legs
- Food
- Grandmother
- Grandfather
- Friends
- Classical music
- Pillows
- Sleep
- Travelling
- Speaking 8 languages
- Intelligence
- Sunglasses
- All my dresses
- Handbags
- Arts
- Paris
- Prague
- Swimming
- Laptop
- Mobile
- Candles
- Matches
- Face creams
- Shampoos
- Pens
- Paper
- Flowers
- Pyjamas
- Tea
- Coffee
- Cooking

Find the Love of Your Life in 30 Days!

- Thai food
- Cherry cake
- Lindt chocolate
- Sausages
- Germany
- Childhood
- Picasso
- Dali
- Barbra Streisand
- George Michael
- Sport cars, etc.

See, it is quite easy to do.

Repeat this exercise as many times as you like.

Because each time you do it, you are going to manifest more great things.

And that is pretty cool!

CASE STUDY

I had a fantastic experience with one of my clients.

I taught her how to be grateful for everything and she kept writing the occasional gratitude journal.

And she noticed that every time she wrote what she is grateful for, a miracle happened that day.

She got so excited that now she writes it down every day and, needless to say, that she is no longer alone, lonely and sad.

His name is Jack!!

CHAPTER 7

Keep Going Until You Get Your Ideal Partner

And now, since you know how to manifest your ideal partner, or SP, you just need to keep going until you physically see him in your 3D reality.

- You need to, first and foremost, know what you want in your ideal partner and keep insisting on him being the version of himself you want in your life
- You create your end scene
- You need to let go
- You have to turn your negative beliefs into positive ones.
- You need to affirm and keep your mental diet.
- You need to understand and believe in manifesting.
- You have to disregard time, competition and circumstances.
- And you need to live in the wish fulfilled. Live *knowing* that they are already with you.

- **And moreover – throughout this time, you need to behave like a winner!!**

And guess what winners never, ever do?

They never give up!!

But what they do successfully is: they keep going no matter what.

A Word about Time

Something we cannot dictate in manifesting is **when** something will happen. If you set deadlines for your manifestation, you usually delay the process. In my experience, it is the 'letting go and not thinking about it' that allows it to happen faster.

Some people give up too early because what they want doesn't happen at the hour they have appointed.

They are, literally, 'dis-appointed'.

Manifesting is not 'one time for all'.

The process of creation is one of trial and error, tweaking and perfecting until you get what YOU want.

There are no *mis*-Takes, as your early designs are just prototypes, like scenes in your movie; Take 1, Take 2, Take 3......until you are completely satisfied with your design.

It's supposed to be Fun!

Remember, you are creating this experience for your pleasure, so enjoy the journey!

CASE STUDY

A client called me one day and she said: "I do love my friend with benefits but I want to give up manifesting him".

So, she came to my office and the first thing I told her was that manifesting never stops.

Manifesting is what makes this world tick.

You can never give up manifesting.

Because, if you do that, you are going to manifest things anyway, but unconsciously, and that is exactly what gives the mixed results we do not like.

After I explained to her that there is no giving up, she changed her story, stopped being desperate for results and he is no longer a friend with benefits.

He now is a boyfriend!

I do love a good ending, don't you?

Winners keep learning, tweaking and believing.

And that is exactly what you need to do if you want your man.

CHAPTER 8

What If The Love Of Your Life Is Already In Your Life?

C an men change?

Absolutely.

Anyone can change.

It irked me my whole life when people kept saying "people do not change".

It is so not true. People change every second of their life. Physically and psychologically.

If other people are reflecting your thoughts, and your thoughts about them change, then they *must* change to reflect those thoughts.

It cannot be otherwise. It's the law.

So, some of you want to manifest an ideal partner they have never met and now you know how to do that.

But, for others, the question is - **can you change the partner you are with?**

And I say YES, YES, YES!!

The only thing I tell clients to take into consideration when they think about manifesting a different, ideal version of their partner, is whether they really want to spend the time and energy doing that.

If your answer is "Yes", then great and let's get on with it.

If the answer is "No", then sometimes it is better to let go and start anew with someone who does not need a major upgrade!

But in all cases, yes, you can change the person you are with or want to be with and know already.

So, remember how we manifest all results including how others behave towards us and how they treat us?

You manifested your partner the way he is.

You did so with your beliefs and experiences of how your parents treated you, how your father treated you, how your previous boyfriends treated you.

You can change all of that.

EXERCISE:
PARTNER TWEAK and REFINE

Write a list of things you do not like about your partner.

What you do not like about them is your manifestation of who you think they are.

So, if you do not like something, turn it around and start manifesting the exact opposite.

CASE STUDY

It is easy to manifest your ex back.

Much easier than you think.

Why? Because you already have a relationship with them really.

They know you, they used to like you and, if you manifested them once, you can manifest them as many times as you would like again.

My client broke up with her ex and came to me for some private coaching, and we had a chat.

It was obvious she could not forgive him for the painful break up.

She created a whole negative story about how nasty he was, how cruel he was and that he did not love her.

After I explained that she manifested the break up by being needy and clingy, and that she needs to take responsibility for her actions, she started changing that story.

She saw him as the person she wanted him to be and guess what?

He showed up a few weeks later.

And this was after she thought that the break up was so bad he may never be back!

You see? Miracles happen every day.

Because we are in charge of making miracles.

Nothing is set in stone, so you have the power to constantly adjust and refine your creations.

- And why wouldn't you? If you are unhappy with some aspect, just give it a tweak.
- Don't believe it can be done?

Try it and see!

Example:

Negative belief: He does not bring me flowers

Positive belief: He brings me flowers all the time.

Negative belief: He does not love me anymore.

Positive belief: He loves me more and more with every day.

Negative belief: He is cheating on me

Positive belief: He only has eyes for me and is the most loyal of men

See how easy it is?

And that is how you recreate your current SP.

Or, when you write your list of 300 things you want in your SP, just keep insisting on all those qualities, affirm them and see what happens.

And if you stop reacting emotionally to his current version and insist on the new one, you will see *enormous* changes almost instantly.

CHAPTER 9

How To Work With Me

By now you should be equipped with all the tools you need to create the love of your life in 30 Days.

The only thing that can stop you is **your own mind.**

Your thoughts, your beliefs.

If you have been running in 'default' mode for most of your life, you may be arguing for your closely-held beliefs or even blind to their existence.

Beliefs such as:

- *Good men are hard to find*
- *Men always let me down – their true colours show eventually*
- *I just have to put up with being disrespected – I'm not worthy of better*
- *I'm too fat, old, ugly, busy, unlucky, short, poor, purple to find a man.*

- *I can never get what I want – I must lower my standards and be happy with whatever shows up.*

These thoughts may be conscious or subconscious, but why would you allow them to continue to keep running the show when you know that you are worthy of so much better?

You are worthy of the love of your life and you have the right to choose them.

I have many years' experience of helping women and men around the world to quickly become powerful conscious **manifestors.**

One on One VIP Coaching:

Let's work together to quickly identify the blocks and start attracting your SP now.

Find The Love of Your Life in 30 Days Video Course:

This course will reveal your blocks and negative beliefs responsible for not being with the ideal partner/SP just yet. It will show you all you ever needed to know about every single step of getting your dream relationship.

Elite Group SP Coaching:

If personal coaching is not within your reach at the moment, here is an exclusive opportunity for you to ask me anything and get to know a fantastic group of people who are manifesting their lives by design.

Jana Green Coaching:

Find the Love of Your Life

Manifest Your Money Dreams

Program Your Brain to Create Your Ideal Body

Become a Master Manifestor: How to have, be or do anything

Find the Love of Your Life in 30 Days!

Jana Green International:

Success Coaching Levels 1, 2 and 3

How to Be a Millionaire

How to Be a Billionaire

Jana Green Institute:

Jana Green USS (Ultrarapid Success System) for coaches, psychologists and therapists

Contact me

Email: jana@janagreen.co.uk

Website: www.janagreeninternational.com

Link - Jana Green Coaching Elite Group |
https://www.facebook.com/groups/mmmepro1

About The Author

Jana Green is an international Success Coach and Mentor. She specializes in the application of science-based success systems, and thought and behavioural modification into personal lives and business growth.

Jana has been featured in CNN and international magazines, she has been a part of an expert panel in the USA with some of the world's coaching royalty and her speeches are followed in 90 countries around the world.

She has extensive experience in successfully coaching and mentoring thousands of clients around the world, including international VIPs, helping them to transform their health, relationships, businesses, finances and much more.

Jana also runs several international "Program Yourself To Be A Winner" groups and has designed coaching programs which help thousands of people transform their lives quickly and successfully.

What Others Are Saying About Jana

"Jana Green changed my life when she was able to accomplish with me in only 3 hours what I have spent decades trying to achieve in therapy. She identified my biggest traumas, deepest buried fears, unresolved emotions and all the blocks standing in the way of me having all my dreams fulfilled. She helped me in the shortest time start turning them all around so I easily and effortlessly began to create the life I had always desired. Jana Green is truly a Superstar!

... an extra special thank-you to Jana Green! Your one-on-one coaching sessions have changed my life and I am now definitely a Master Manifestor thanks to you."

Kirsty Bostock, Psychologist, Brisbane, Australia

"Jana Green, you are f*****g brilliant...we had a conversation on Friday about my SP and you told me to stop interfering with the middle, it knows more than I do, to let it go and it will happen. OMG...guess who showed up the same day... my SP. Guess who asked me to come over and who wants to do a weekend getaway...my SP...OMG! Thank you, Jana, you rock!"

Dianne Kelson, Ohio, USA

"Jana taught me about self-concept, self-respect, self-love and showed me how to manifest properly. I am now in a brand-new relationship with an amazing man, who appreciates and respects me fully. Thanks again Jana!"

Margo Baxter, Entrepreneur, Ireland

"Jana helped change my mindset towards men! Even more towards myself. I learnt to love myself more and know what I deserve… I met my special one and we are building a future together! Am so thankful…!"

Maria Adamides, London, UK

Made in United States
Orlando, FL
25 March 2025

59845689R00062